What's Wrong with Dad?

Amanda Mayers

Published by
Chipmunkapublishing
United Kingdom

http://www.chipmunkapublishing.com

Email: NanaMandy1967@gmail.com

About Chipmunkapublishing

Mental health books give a voice to writers with mental illness around the world. At Chipmunkapublishing we raise awareness of mental health and the stigma surrounding mental health problems by encouraging society to listen. We are documenting mental health literature as a genre so history does not forget the survivors and carers of people with mental illness and disabilities.

What’s Wong with Dad? is part of the Feelings Series

Dedicate to my son's Michael and Kristian

Any profits will go to the work of NSPCC'S Childline.

Michael was lay crying on his bed. He was so upset because his dad had shouted at him.

Michael knew his dad was poorly and sometimes his dad thought strange things and spoke to people who nobody else could see. Michael was so upset because he had tried to be such a good big boy all day.

'Dad has so many people helping him; I wish I could talk to someone' said Michael out loud.

At that moment Michael could see a shimmering light in his bedroom. Suddenly a figure appeared.

‘Who are you?!’ he said in amazement as he dried his eyes.

‘I am the Feelings Fairy, most people call me Bob the Guru’, announced the tall round man with a long ginger beard, with a small box in one hand and a bag of colourful stones in the other.

‘Why are you here?’ asked Michael.

‘You are such a special young man, that I thought could do with a bit of help; that’s my job you see, to help young people whose mums or dads are troubled,’ said Bob.

‘What do you mean troubled?’ asked Michael.

‘I work with young people whose parents have mental health problems’ said Bob the Guru.

‘Some people call my dad mental, that really upsets me and makes me angry. Sometimes they call him ‘schizo,’ and it really hurts my feelings-I love my dad'.

'What do they mean 'schizo?' Asked Michael.

Bob replied, 'most people use that word to upset other people. They usually don't know what it means except that a person may be confused at times and may not make a lot of sense.'

'Is my dad 'schizo?' asked Michael.

'Your dad has a mental illness called Schizophrenia' replied Bob the Guru.

‘I know that dad gets suspicious about people and thinks they’re talking about him- mum says that he can get paranoid, she says that this is the word to describe how he’s feeling’.

‘Dad sometimes thinks he can talk to ghosts, he calls them spirits’.

‘I know when dad’s not too well, when he puts his headphones on to listen to his music’. ‘Mum says that he hears voices of people who aren’t there and sometimes he hears the telephone or doorbell ringing when nobody’s there’, said Michael

‘These are called hallucinations. They are part of your dads illness, sometimes he may feel that he can smell things that nobody else can smell, or feel like he’s being touched when there may be nobody in the room with him’, said Bob the Guru

‘Why does this happen?’ asked a puzzled Michael.

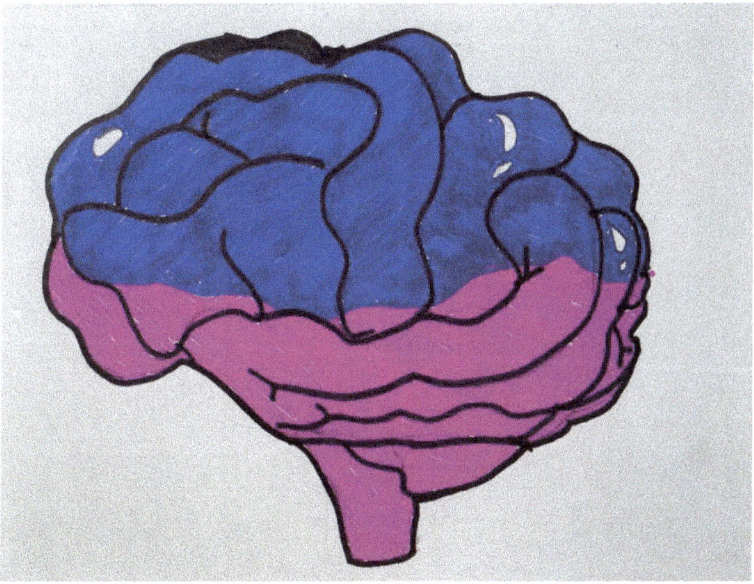

‘Well, you see the brain is a very complex organ, this means that it is very hard to understand. People with Schizophrenia have chemicals that aren’t working properly in their brains, and they can have paranoid thoughts, as well as hallucinations and these changes can affect their mood by making hem happy or sad, angry or agitated or even frightened', said Bob.

'I feel all those feelings; do I have Schizophrenia?' Michael quizzed Bob.

'No, you don't, all your feelings are very natural considering what you are going through with your dads illness, and I am here to help you manage those feelings so that you are not unhappy,' Bob advised Michael.

‘How can you make me happy when my dad has to go into hospital?’ said Michael defiantly.

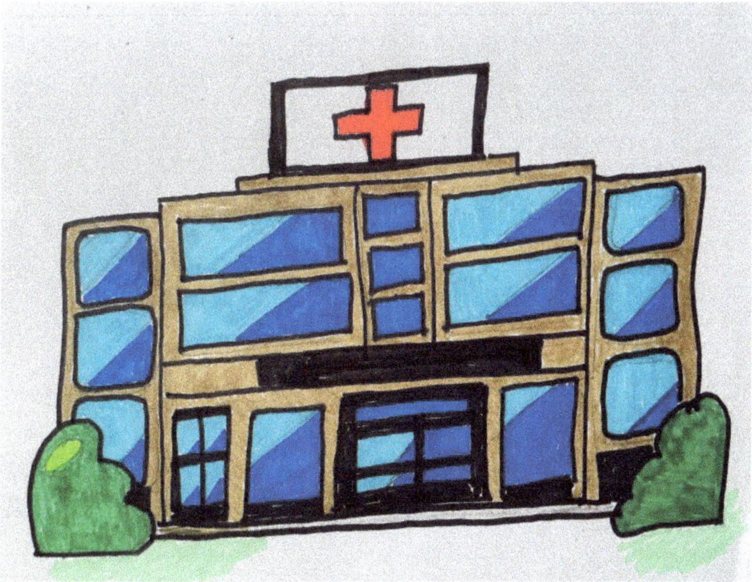

‘If the mental health doctors who are called psychiatrists and the nurses and social workers think that is the best place to get your dad better then I would hope that your dad would be in a safe place and that he would get better faster than at home, so he could return home soon and be a good dad again’, said Bob.

EMERGENCY AMBULANCE

'Why does dad have to take tablets all the time?' asked Michael.

‘Some people with Schizophrenia must take tablets to make the chemicals in their brain work better to stop the paranoia and hallucinations’, said Bob the Guru.

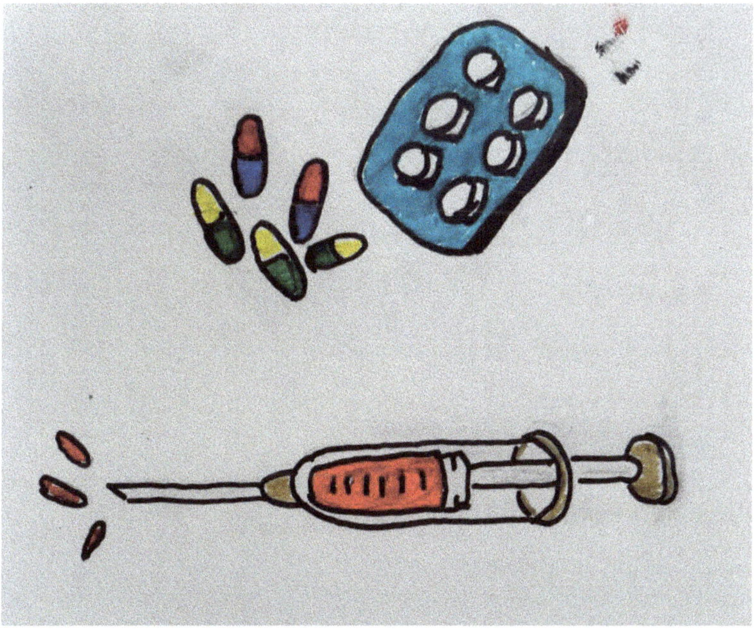

‘Dad used to have injections off his nurse what were they for then?’ asked Michael.

‘They would be off his community psychiatric nurse, sometimes called a CPN for short. The injections work in the same way as your dads tablets. Sometimes injections are given if a person keeps forgetting to take the tablets or maybe feels better and they think they don’t need the tablets,’ said Bob

‘How do you feel now?’ asked Bob the Guru.

‘Well, I’m still upset, not as angry, but still annoyed at my dads illness and at nasty people poking fun at him behind his back', said Michael.

'Well let me just say that your dad is a grown up and when he is well, he can probably laugh off other people's jibes, and he would be upset that it had bothered you. What I would suggest is that you take this small box and these colourful stones that I have brought you and every time you have a worry, or are angry or sad, put a stone in the box. What I will do is visit you every night whilst you are asleep and I will check the box; I will sprinkle special glitter dust on them which is invisible to the human eye, and this will soak up all the pain that you are feeling' said Bob the Guru reassuringly.

'The next day the stones can be used again if you need them', said Bob

'If you need to talk about how you are feeling there are many people who will be more than happy to listen, they could be a teacher, your dads CPN or Social Worker or you might even be able to talk to a special family worker'.

POLICE

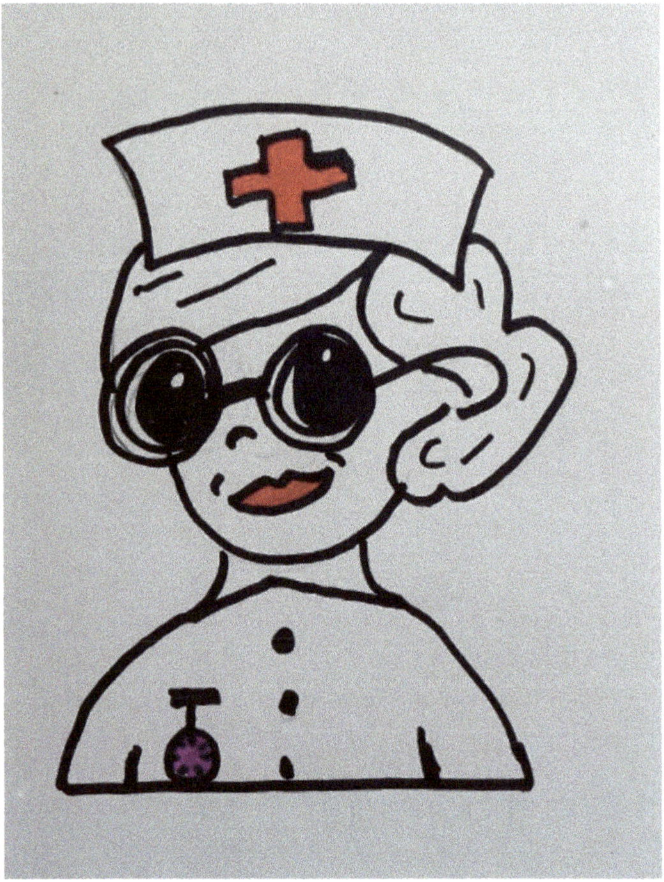

‘I will always be listening to you although you may not see me and I will be checking your box every night', said Bob.

Michael took the box and the bag of colourful stones and started to put a stone for each upsetting feeling or worry into the box. He then placed the box under his pillow.

'Well goodnight
Master Michael,' said Bob the Feelings Fairy otherwise known as Bob the Guru.

'Goodnight Bob,' said Micheal as he climbed under the covers and into bed.

That night Michael slept soundly. Bob the Guru did come, and he sprinkled his invisible dust on the stones, just as he said he would.

The next morning Michael awoke much happier as though a weight had been lifted off his mind. From that night on, Michael put fewer stones into his box to have the invisible dust, spread by Bob the Guru, soak up the bad feelings.

Michael often said out loud in his room what each stone meant, just in case Bob was listening (which he most certainly was!)

www.ingramcontent.com/pod-product-compliance
Lightning Source LLC
LaVergne TN
LVHW050924210926
848482LV00012B/534
* 9 7 8 1 7 8 3 8 2 8 0 2 9 *